Ronaldo

THE MAKING OF THE BEST

LARRY EDWARDS

RONALDO THE MAKING OF THE BEST

Who Is Cristiano Ronaldo?

Ever since the European Championships in 2004, the equivalent of the Gold Cup for European teams, Cristiano Ronaldo has been one of the hottest properties in world football. Having established himself at Manchester United as a player of real quality, Ronaldo has since become one of the greatest players of all-time for Real Madrid, his boyhood team.

For the last ten years, he has been the model for any wide player or forward to base themselves upon. Even as a youngster at Sporting Lisbon of Portugal & Manchester United, Ronaldo was an accomplished soccer player who understood both his role in the team, and the progression of the game.

LARRY EDWARDS

RONALDO THE MAKING OF THE BEST

Why Is He So Well Known?

Ronaldo has lived many dreams already, and his career is nowhere near finished. He has been one of the most inspiring soccer players of his generation, and goes down in the all-time list of the best soccer players ever. But what makes Cristiano Ronaldo so good? Why is he the example for any forward player?

We want to look into his background, his skill set, and why he is such a big influence in sports. If you want to base yourself around a specific soccer player, then few are better to use as your model than Cristiano Ronaldo. He has, at the time of writing, scored 186 league goals for Real Madrid, in just 169 games!

For reference, a good record for a top class striker is around one goal every 2 games. Ronaldo is currently better than a goal every single game. This type of

LARRY EDWARDS

goalscoring has not been witnessed in the top European leagues for many years, and he has certainly helped to buck a trend and show the world just how good a soccer player can be.

Does this sound like the type of role model that any aspiring soccer player should have?

RONALDO THE MAKING OF THE BEST

The Complete Soccer Player

There are many things to admire about Cristiano Ronaldo – his pace, his physique, his work rate and his shooting have all been wildly praised for many years. He's one of the quickest players in the world, and his strength & power both on the ball and off the ball make him an incredible asset either up front as a striker, or in a wide position.

LARRY EDWARDS

Mental Endurance & Determination

However, it's his incredible determination to improve that makes Ronaldo stand out so much. Whether it's been his ability to work as a teammate, his passing, his long-range shooting, his free-kicks or his heading Ronaldo has visibly improved on many aspects of his game since he was young. Many soccer players will progress very little outside of becoming more consistent as they get older, and don't add too many new tricks or additions to their game.

However, Ronaldo bucks this trend massively with an incredible determination to get it right more often than not when he is involved in a soccer game. While always blessed with amazing skills and natural talent, Ronaldo has actively improved weaknesses in his game to become a more rounded soccer player – if somebody as clearly gifted as Ronaldo is willing to work this hard to improve then so should every young soccer player!

Developed & Improved

If you watch videos of Cristiano Ronaldo as a youngster, he looks a completely different player to the one that you see every weekend for Real Madrid. While he was at one point a tricky winger who was a little selfish, and poor in the air, today he is one of the best aerial strikers in the game. His ability to play all across the front, and do each job perfectly well, is a huge asset for both himself and his teammates.

If you want to be a successful soccer player today, you have to be versatile. Systems are always changing around you and new ways of playing area always evolving, and it's important to be able to adapt to each and every style that you are asked to by a manager or a coach.

The First To Defend

Ronaldo does this seamlessly, and will play anywhere for his team and give his same output. Even his mentality & work rate have improved over the years – he now presses defences much better, and regularly wins back possession for his team just by being insistent.

A Global Name

The huge amounts of media attention that Cristiano Ronaldo is put under is incredible — he is easily one of the most commonly watched and written about soccer players of all-time. Everybody knows who he is, and what he is capable of. Even people who hate soccer will be able to say that they know Ronaldo is one of the best in the world!

This huge profile brings a massive amount of fans to his domain — his official Twitter account, @cristiano, currently has 30m followers — and thousands of youngsters who look up to him. Therefore, his personality is as important as his ability on the pitch, and it's safe to say that Ronaldo is a kind-hearted individual who has taken part in various charitable ventures in his time.

100% Commitment

This helps his image further, and when you put it together with his immense appetite for training and working hard it's hard to find a more suitable player in the whole of the world to be so popular. Cristiano Ronaldo is also well acclaimed within the sport because he does not drink alcohol – although it's widely accepted that alcohol in moderation is acceptable, to be the best you need to be willing to make sacrifices.

He also donated a huge sum of money - £100,000 – to his hometown in Portugal, Madeira, so that they could build a cancer centre on the island. It's this hugely positive image that helps push Ronaldo even further up in people's opinions – he is a selfless individual who looks after others before himself.

His Harshest Critics

This does bring his fair share of detractors, though. Many people are happy to abuse and mock Ronaldo when he suffers or fails on or off the pitch. It's easy to mock the best, though, right? Because when they fail it's so rare you really do want to make the most of the situation!

Needless to say that Ronaldo's positive image and obvious attraction to hard work and being a determined member of his team pays off far more than those who look to abuse and insult him. He is the perfect role model.

RONALDO   THE MAKING OF THE BEST

How Good Is Ronaldo?

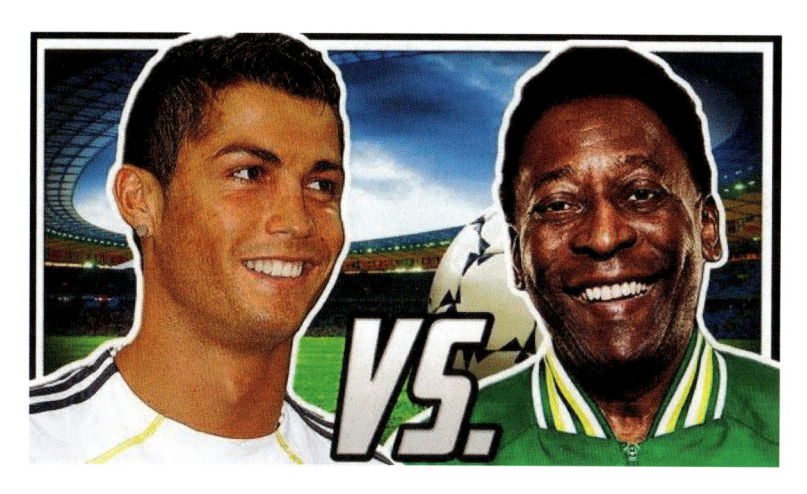

Comparing Cristiano Ronaldo to the other great names of world football is hard. When you look at guys like Diego Maradona, Pele or Alfredo di Stefano, they never had the same physique or pace as Ronaldo possesses today. They also led different lives to what Ronaldo does – it's much easier to compare Ronaldo with the greats of the modern era.

He is currently the top scorer of all time for Portugal, overtaking greats like Rui Costa & Luis Figo along the way. He is also one of the highest scorers of all time for his club side, Real Madrid. In terms of comparing him with players he has played with, he is by far and away the best of his generation. He is easily on a par in terms of class as anybody in the game, with only Lionel Messi being able to rival him for accolades in the same time as a player.

LARRY EDWARDS

RONALDO   THE MAKING OF THE BEST

What About Messi?

Messi is one of the finest players in the world as well, and has won many trophies with Barcelona. It has been a neck-and-neck contest ever since 2008 between the two to see who the best player in the world is individually, and both are the ideal model for any young player who wants to emulate either. It all depends, really – how tall are you? If you are nice and tall then Ronaldo should be your role model!

Who's Better?

It's easy enough to say though that both Messi & Ronaldo will go down as possible the greatest players of all time, and it might just come down to who wins the most in their last years as soccer players! Either way, though, Ronaldo is the finest product of the Portuguese football system of all times and arguably the greatest European player of all time.

His amazing determination to improving is only bettered by his infectious personality and ability to change a game and inspire his entire team to do better on the field. If you want to be a better soccer player, then using the likes of Cristiano Ronaldo as your role model could be one of the smartest things that you have ever done!

His use of his pace and height makes him a more complete addition to the team than Messi, because he offers more to a direct style of football when his team needs a quick goal or two. But when it comes to trophies won, Messi is still out in front with some amazing seasons behind him.

Using the best as the basis for your own development is the ideal way to get better – and with Ronaldo, you can be sure that only a handful of players in all-time history can come close.

From the Author

Thank you very much for downloading and reading this book. I hope that you find the information useful and interesting.

If you enjoyed the book, please take a moment to share your opinion with other on the book page at
http://www.amazon.com/dp/B00NYL3I6U

Still craving for more interesting soccer books? I recommend you to check out my other soccer books below that are also available for a great price.

RONALDO — THE MAKING OF THE BEST

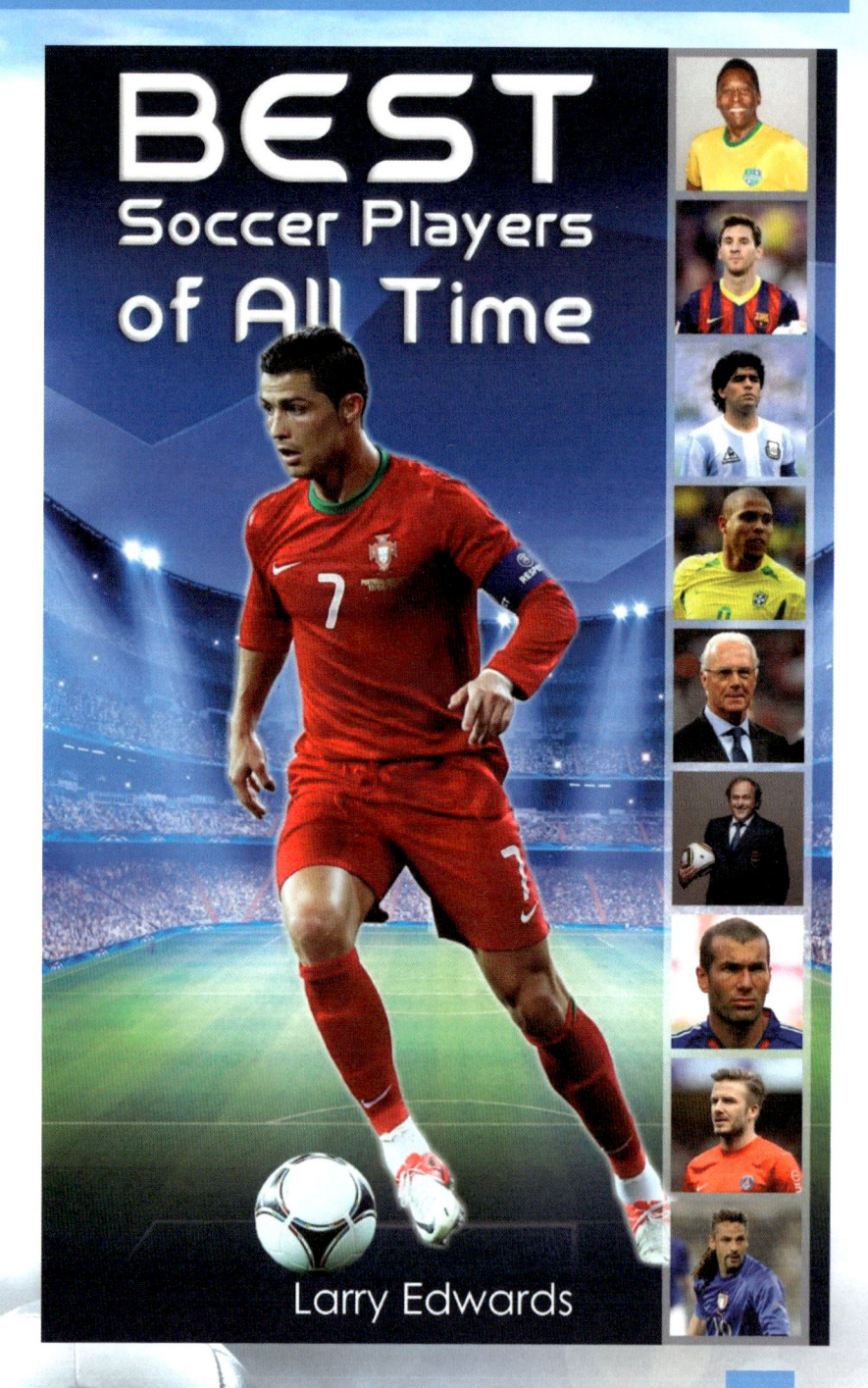

RONALDO THE MAKING OF THE BEST

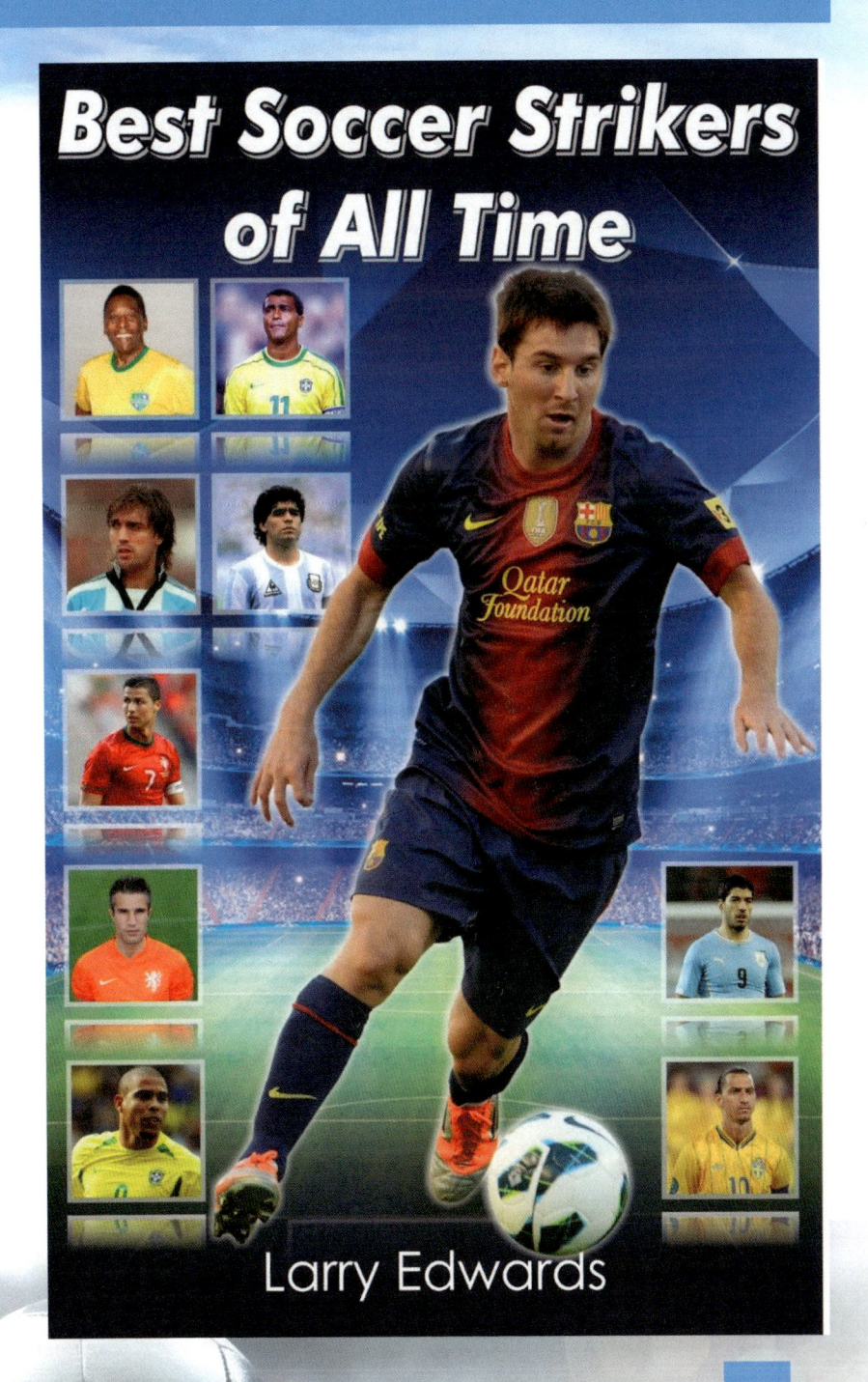

Best Soccer Strikers of All Time

Larry Edwards

LARRY EDWARDS 18

RONALDO — THE MAKING OF THE BEST

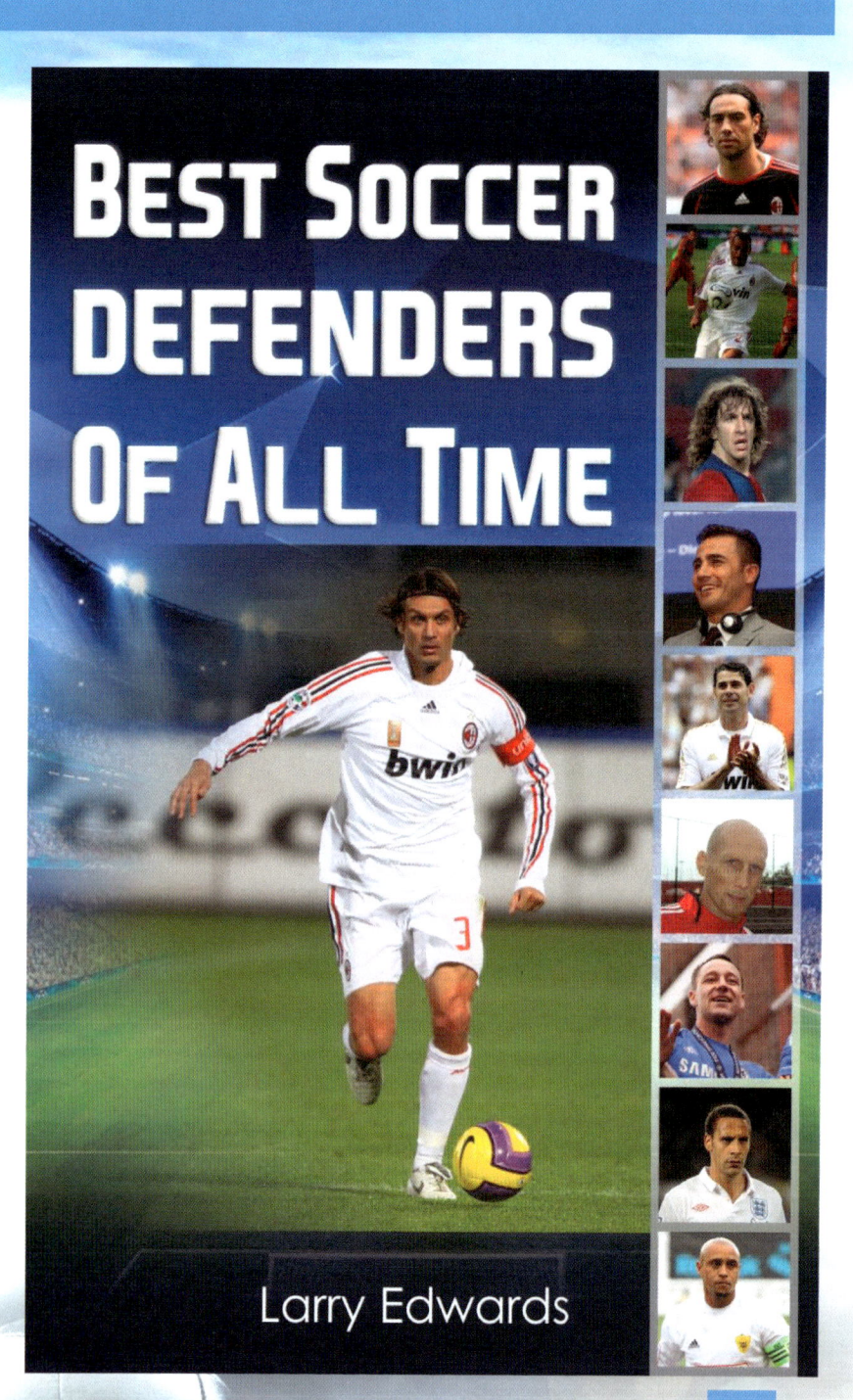

Best Soccer Defenders Of All Time

Larry Edwards

LARRY EDWARDS 19

RONALDO　　　　　　　　　THE MAKING OF THE BEST

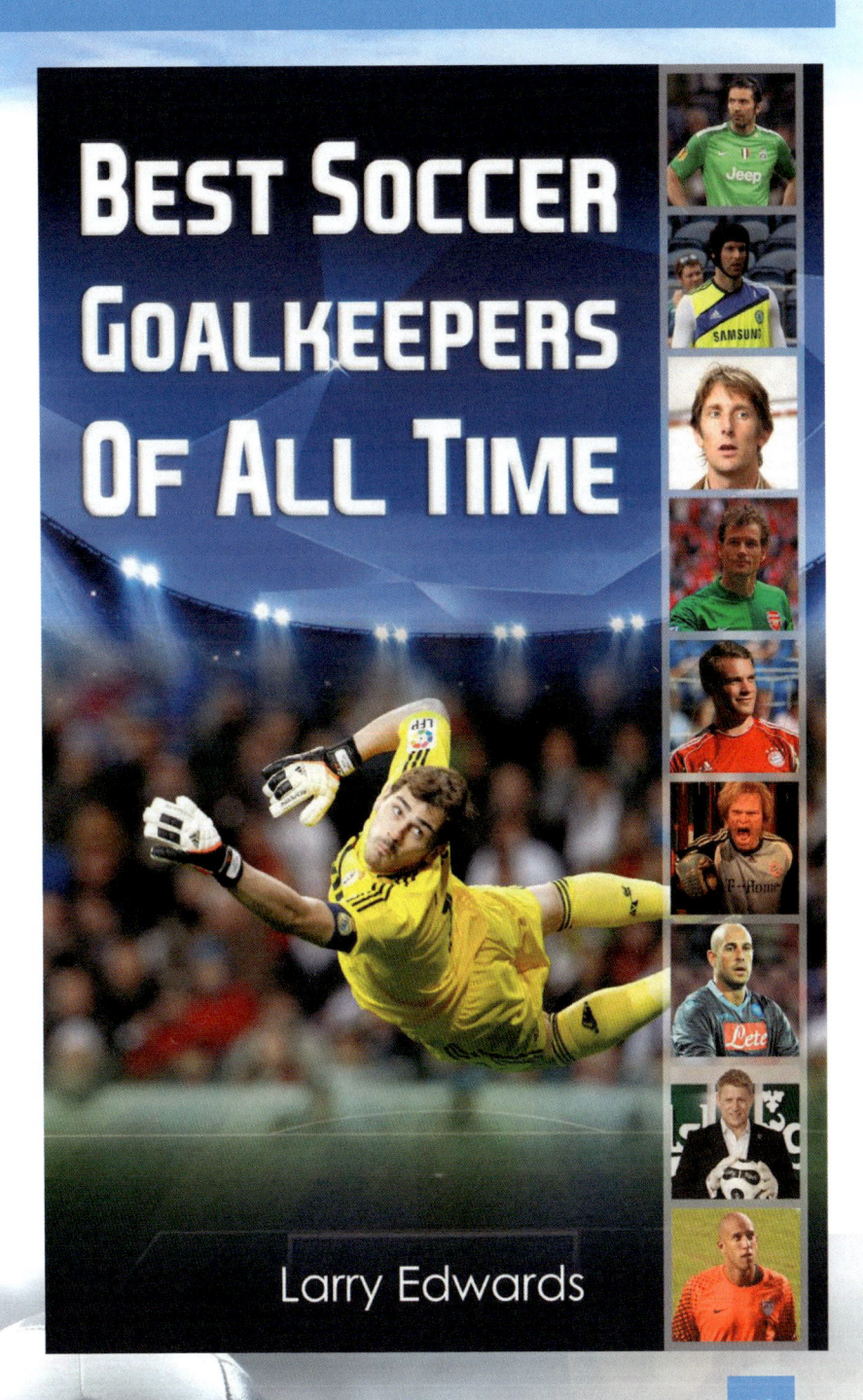

Best Soccer Goalkeepers Of All Time

Larry Edwards

LARRY EDWARDS　20

RONALDO — THE MAKING OF THE BEST

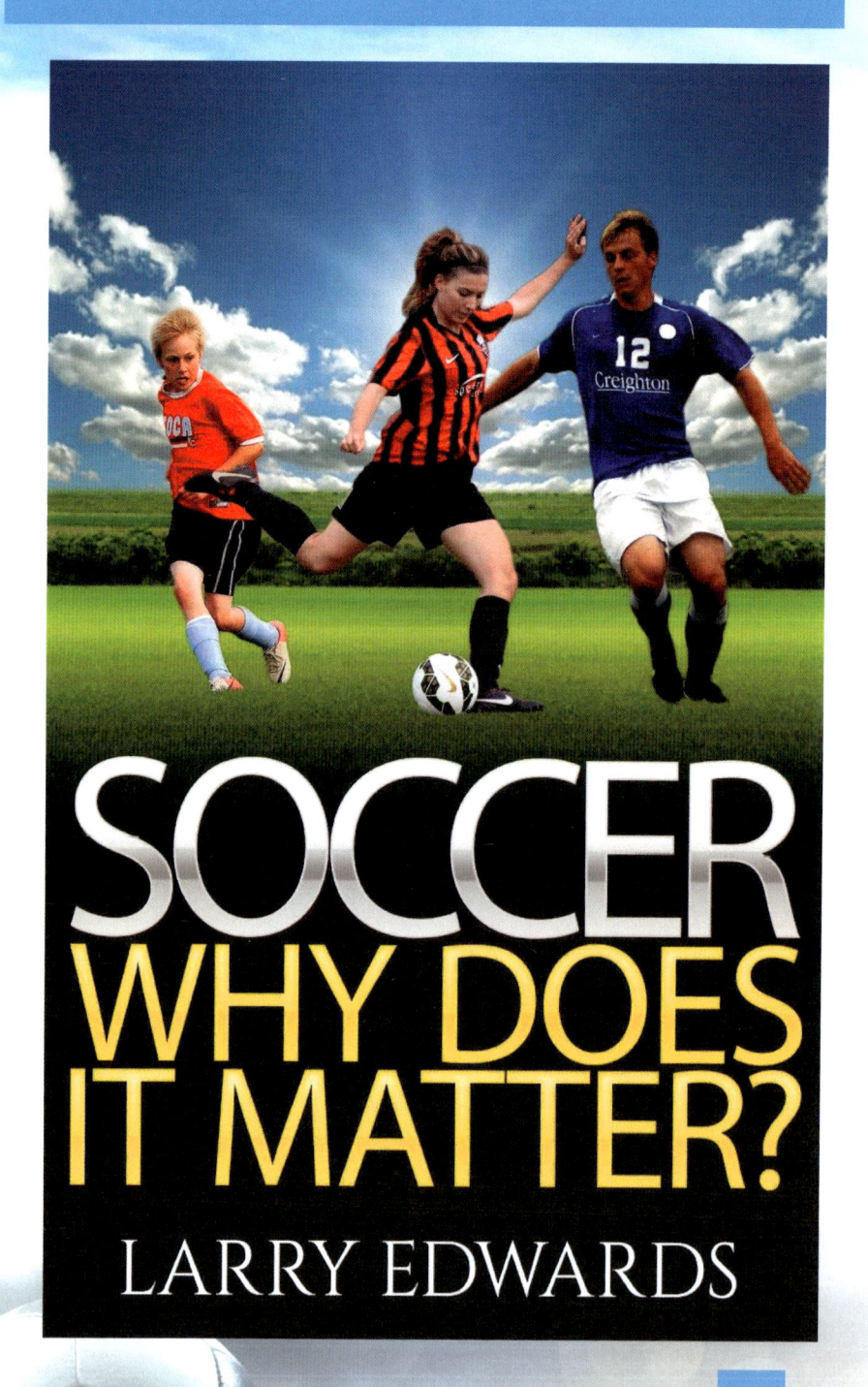

SOCCER
WHY DOES IT MATTER?

LARRY EDWARDS

LARRY EDWARDS | 21

RONALDO — THE MAKING OF THE BEST

MESSI
Best Of The Best
Larry Edwards

LARRY EDWARDS 22

| RONALDO | THE MAKING OF THE BEST |

NEYMAR

The Path to Becoming the Best

Larry Edwards

LARRY EDWARDS | 23

How To BECOME A GOOD SOCCER PLAYER

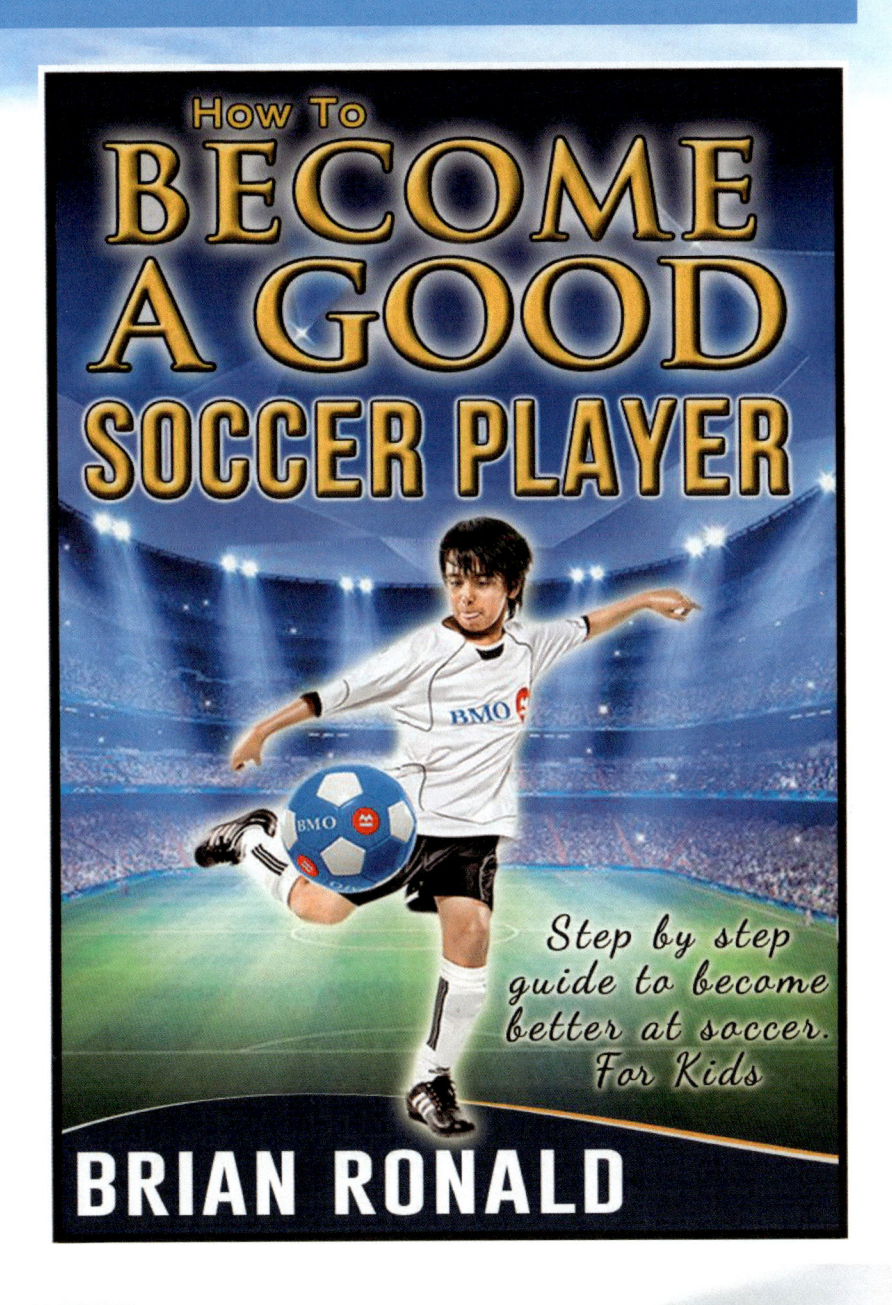

Step by step guide to become better at soccer. For Kids

BRIAN RONALD

Copyright

Copyright © 2014 by Larry Edwards.

All rights reserved. No part of this publication may be reproduced, distributed, or transmitted in any form or by any means, including photocopying, recording, or other electronic or mechanical methods, without the prior written permission of the publisher, except in the case of brief quotations embodied in critical reviews and certain other noncommercial uses permitted by copyright law.

Made in the USA
Lexington, KY
02 December 2015